T0147235

Portals of Peace

A Path to Inner Peace and a Healed World

Kimberly Kingsley

iUniverse, Inc.
New York   Bloomington

Portals of Peace
A Path to Inner Peace and a Healed World

Cover designed by Sarah Loukota

iUniverse books may be ordered through booksellers or by contacting:

*iUniverse
1663 Liberty Drive
Bloomington, IN 47403
www.iuniverse.com
1-800-Authors (1-800-288-4677)*

*Because of the dynamic nature of the Internet, any Web addresses or
links contained in this book may have changed since publication and may
no longer be valid.*

*ISBN: 978-1-4401-4139-3 (pbk)
ISBN: 978-1-4401-4140-9 (ebk)*

Printed in the United States of America

iUniverse rev. date: 4/28/2009

Contents

Introduction

Several years ago, while I was occupied with other projects, I received a vision. It was an image of Earth from space. Portals of light were opening up on its surface, one after another, sending shafts of light streaming out into the cosmos. As patches of our globe lit up, the process accelerated. This became the vision for *Portals of Peace*. As we open up from the inside and allow our light to fully shine, a new era of peace blankets the world. The time for this vision is now, as the group of individuals willing to enlist in the army of light grows bigger every day.

The original seeds for this book, and my life's work in general, were planted at the age of twenty-seven when I had a spiritual awakening that changed my life. I had just moved from Phoenix where I grew up, to downtown Chicago where everything was fresh and unfamiliar. I was open to whatever life had to offer, and it turns out life had a great deal to offer. Shortly after arriving in the big city perched on the edge of a huge expanse of sparkling water, I stumbled upon *A Course in Miracles* through a newspaper review of Marianne Williamson's book, *A Return to Love* (a wonderful introduction to *The Course*). I immediately recognized this new way of looking at the world as *truth* and proceeded to cry for three days. The tears of relief were only the beginning of my personal transformation, but something had fundamentally shifted in my core, and I was awake for the first time in my life. The experience was profound and deep – on a cellular level. Prior to the awakening, I was living in the dark, trying to find my way without any direction. I was tormented with inner struggles that left me completely void of inner peace. This "eye-opening" time restored my sanity and changed the course of my life.

I'm not alone in this experience. Right now, many of us are waking up to the true nature of life. Some of us awaken spontaneously upon recognizing the truth or after going through a life-changing event, while others open to truth gradually, like a blossoming flower.

My life's work has centered upon teaching the timeless principles that lead to inner peace. Not until several years ago however, did I realize that inner peace has a profound and literal connection to world peace. While I'm aware of the wide-spread rhetoric surrounding the idea that inner peace leads to world peace, I'm not aware of many step-by-step guides on how to get there. *Portals of Peace*, while not the only path, reveals a direct and concrete approach to inner peace and ultimately world peace. Inner peace does not equal happiness. I believe most of us consider ourselves to be happy. Inner peace results from a complete integration of self, which involves partially undoing of the effects of socialization. In other words, becoming more of who we are and less of who we think we "should" be in order to fit in.

This book is geared toward the committed aspirant, seeker, self-help enthusiast, and activist – as only those who are entirely dedicated to doing their part in making this world a better place will be inspired to follow the path outlined in the pages that follow.

It is my belief that the world is ready to take a quantum leap toward becoming a more love-based community, and that those of us willing to "feel the burn" of transformation will usher in this unprecedented era.

I am grateful for each reader who walks this sometimes difficult, but ultimately inspiring journey, as each step taken widens the path to peace.

Chapter 1
Peace

I've never talked to a person who wasn't for world peace. Sometimes the cry for peace gets louder and sometimes it fades to a hum for a while. But even when the issue isn't on the forefront, peace is a deeply held value shared by all of humanity. The activists of the '60s not only cried out for peace, they marched, they spoke, and they got arrested. They did everything in their power to transform a world that they knew was out of balance, and yet here we are again, with a new wave of people crying out, marching and shouting for peace. We sense the futility of conflict and war, and those of us who are awake will always stand up and try to make things right.

Why then, when passionate, intelligent people do everything in their power to cultivate peace, doesn't it work? Why is it that the landscape of violence changes, but the violence itself never goes away?

Right now there is a diverse group of people on the planet dedicated to ushering in a more peaceful era. If you have picked up this book, you are among them. They range in age – many are the same visionary baby boomer men and women who called for peace in the sixties. Others, in their 20s, 30s and 40s are going to music festivals and voting for change. The tenor of the group is unmistakable – each of these peace seeking individuals is passionate, full of life and committed to doing whatever is necessary to birth a more peaceful world.

What you are about to read is a radical approach to world peace. It is radical because it calls for you to impeccably represent on the inside that which you are seeking on the outside. A portal of peace is one who uses his or her warrior spirit to unite rather than divide. Here's the catch – *it is your presence that unites, not your beliefs, words or actions.*

There is a reason that conflict prevails, despite the fact that almost all people desire peace in their homes, schools and in the world. The reason is that conflict in the world is a direct reflection of conflict within oneself that is projected outward. It is important to note that projection of conflict operates on two levels: individual and collective. The collective psyche, or collective consciousness, reflects the mindset of the masses. It is the collective psyche that perpetuates conflict on the world's stage, while conflict (or peace) in one's immediate environment is a reflection of the individual's mindset.

The collective consciousness is a force field that pulls the world into alignment with its beliefs. Its magnetic force is difficult for any one person – no matter how brilliant or visionary – to penetrate. Groups of people however – even fairly small groups – can and do affect this field all the time.

The concept of collective consciousness has been around for a long time. Until recently however, it has been no more than a theory. There is now evidence of this field, which validates its power and presence. A good source on this subject is Robert Kenny, an author and professor at the California Institute of Integral Studies. He has written a number of articles on collective consciousness, including a comprehensive paper, What Can Science Tell Us About Collective Consciousness and Collective Wisdom? (http://www.collectivewisdominitiative.org/papers/kenny_science.htm). In the paper he explores the studies that measure the impact that groups can have on collective consciousness. After careful review of the research, Kenny states:

> These and other studies provide strong evidence that, given certain conditions, we can develop and work with our collective consciousness to produce a number of important interpersonal, organizational and social benefits: increased empathy, compassion, understanding, respect, appreciation and rapport; greater cooperation, creative collaboration, teamwork and collective wisdom; and enhanced well-being, peace, and physical, emotional, mental and spiritual health. In our increasingly diverse workplaces, communities and global institutions, where we are challenged by extremely complex problems, developing these capacities will not only pro-

mote the common good, but could also ensure our survival.

Once enough of us experience true inner peace, the collective consciousness will shift to refect that. So here we are, at a point in history when more people than ever are willing to do whatever it takes to bring about peace. The "whatever it takes" is contained in this book.

Chapter 2
The Inner Divide

Bob is a good man. He loves his wife and kids, he works hard and pays his taxes. People call him a big softy because of how sentimental he gets when he talks of his childhood on the farm. Bob loves baseball and he stands as tall as anyone during the National Anthem, holding his hand firmly on his heart.

But just like everyone else, Bob had some hard times as a kid. His parents divorced when he was seven and it was bitter. He rarely got to see his dad, and to this day can't decide if he's angry at his father or just pities him. He was a big kid, some would say chubby, and the other boys had no problem making him the butt of their jokes. Bob laughed along with them, but on the inside he felt embarrassed and ashamed. Sometimes he would get really angry and feel like he wanted to punch Johnny – the one who was most obnoxious about it all. Bob's best friends were the two cows on their family farm – primarily cared for by his grandfather after his dad left. Bucket and Bess didn't sing songs about his being "fat," and they listened to his every word – they even seemed to enjoy his jokes.

Bob would tell you that the worst day of his life was when he came home from school to find out that the cows had been sold. Yes, his family needed the money to keep a roof over their heads and food on the table, but Bob didn't get that. He was nine at the time, and he would have just as soon slept in the barn and eaten hay for dinner as to give up those cows. He was devastated. All he wanted to do was cry, but when he did, his mother told him that he was the man of the house and that he had to be strong. So for his mother, Bob put on a strong face and acted like everything was okay.

If you were to talk to Bob's wife Vicky, she would tell you that Bob doesn't listen to her enough. That he doesn't "feel" her or empathize with her concerns. Yeah, he tries to offer solutions, but he has a hard time connecting with her in a way that feels intimate. He sometimes even gets angry and blows up when Vicky becomes upset and tells him she needs more intimacy.

Having a soft spot for children and animals and knowing what it feels like to be treated unfairly, Bob has no patience for people who are violent. This overflows into his politics, as he can't stand ruthless dictators. Whenever he witnesses cruelty, his old anger starts to flare and he feels like he's going to pop from the intensity. After a few beers, Bob's been known to say, "We should just bomb the entire middle east."

It doesn't take a psychoanalyst to see that Bob is divided inside. He was trained to deny his feelings, as many of us are, and one cannot sit on the energy of feelings without constructing a sturdy wall to keep them out of awareness. On one side of the wall is Bob's presenting self. He's fun loving and a hard worker. Of course he has his moments, but don't we all?

On the other side of the wall is Bob's repressed self. The feelings of sadness, anger and shame are now heavy and dark because they are so compressed. Each time they threaten to surface, Bob distracts himself with a big meal or a few beers until the overwhelming energy retreats back to the other side of the wall where it is out of sight and once again out of mind. When this doesn't work, Bob explodes with anger and adds to his stockpile of heavy emotion that is constantly trying to make itself heard.

We could just as easily have profiled Bob's wife Vicky – as her psyche is split as well. Learning from an early age how important it is to be kind and loving, she mastered the art of being pleasant, and anything that threatened her likable reputation was pushed aside with as much vigilance as Bob pushes away his undesirable feelings. Unlike Bob, Vicky was allowed to be vulnerable, so sadness is not a feeling she has buried. Vicky's "dark side" is comprised mostly of power and anger – the very emotions that, if exposed, might show the world that she isn't as nice as they think.

Activists, religious zealots and other well meaning individuals can and do project their inner division onto the world as well. It is important to keep in mind that any time a part of oneself is buried – whether it's dark, compressed

while this movement encouraged men to engage in rituals connecting them to their inherent sense of adventure and strength, we still have a long way to go in terms of integrating suppressed emotions. The evolved man has enough space for both fierce masculinity and the expression of feelings. Perhaps the self-help and spirituality movement has provided a gender neutral arena for men and women to continue what was started four decades ago. One current voice on this issue is Terrence Real, author of *How Can I Get through to You: Reconnecting Men and Women.* Real teaches men how to become more relational by learning to reconnect with their feelings. He also works with women to become more empowered, which, as we know, is the other side of the issue.

A whole and healthy psyche, regardless of a person's gender, has a fully developed masculine side and feminine side. The feminine side receives and nurtures, while the masculine side defends and moves forth to achieve what it needs to survive and thrive. As the human race evolves, more of us are becoming whole individuals, able to receive life energy and then protect it so that it can fulfill its function of extending forth.

Aside from the social influences which tend to suppress feelings in men and strength in women, as Bob illustrates, each of us has our own trauma added to the side of the wall that is out of sight.

Once there is a wall between the presenting self and the repressed self, there are factors that make integration challenging, one of which stems from our own physiology.

Physiology

Homeostasis (constant stability in the midst of a rapidly changing environment) is one of the miracles of nature and a feature of any complex system. The human body is one such system – an open system – that interacts with a constantly changing environment while remaining stable within. For example, if you go out into the cold, your internal body temperature remains the same through an increase of circulation and shivering, which generates heat in the cells. Under extreme conditions when the body can no longer maintain its temperature, serious complications and death can occur. Therefore, while our biological systems are brilliant at keeping us stable through various involuntary physical responses, as just mentioned, a severe imbalance can lead to death. For this reason – and it is a good one – the body clings to homeostasis and the status quo. In many ways, this sense of equilibrium is responsible for our resilience and ability to survive, but can also undermine the desire to change – even when the change is healthy.

Another element of survival, and equally as important as homeostasis, is the ability to adapt and evolve to changing environments. We'll refer to this evolutionary process as transformation, because it involves cellular change. There always seems to be tension between these two brothers: Homeostasis sinks his heals in at the first sign of change, while evolution or transformation urges periodic renewal. This tension is present both within us and within the open systems we inhabit, such as our relationships, families and the organizations in which we work. These complex systems resist change in an effort to remain stable, but need to grow and evolve in order to thrive.

Becoming a portal of peace involves evolution and growth and it is important to know the various forces that make change difficult. The physiological dance between homeostasis and transformation can be side-stepped once you know what's happening. The best way to overcome this tension is to move slowly and in harmony with the nudges of your inner self. The psyche rarely transforms in a flash, but once a person stops unconsciously resisting their personal evolution, it begins to move toward wholeness – organically and at the perfect pace.

Chapter 3
The Socialized Psyche

Let's look at Bob as an example of an open system in which the tension between homeostasis and transformation plays itself out. Bob is used to the way he feels inside. Despite the fact that some of his behaviors are not ideal, Bob is fine with who he is. In fact, when old emotions begin to surface and demand attention, Bob doesn't feel right. He feels off balance, which is why he soothes himself with food and beer while using television as a distraction. In this way Bob preserves a sense of inner harmony by holding on to patterns that are familiar and safe.

The life energy or spiritual substance that animates Bob however, is suffocating. Extension is life's primary function – regardless of whether it flows through a human being, a flower or a tree – giving or extension is the fundamental purpose of life. It is how life sustains itself, joins with itself, creates, plays, and reproduces. Therefore, the life energy within Bob continuously seeks to move through him, but consistently bumps into his repressed self. This is not a problem for the life within him, being that it is the great transformative substance. Life could easily burn through the repressed energy and extend through Bob and into the world, but each time it starts to bubble up and dissolve the blocks, Bob aborts the process to maintain his sense of balance.

The question then arises: Who is Bob? Is he the part of his identity that he presents to the world and tries with all his might to preserve, or is he the life energy that animates his cells and seeks to flow through him?

I call this division between presenting self and suppressed self *the socialized psyche.* Arriving into adulthood with buried trauma and a highly evolved set of defense mechanisms to keep it in place (homeostasis) is the natural outcome of socialization. The socialized psyche contains the presenting self, which is out in the open where everyone can see, and the suppressed self that lives in the shadows. The only time we get a glimpse of what lives in the shadows is when it becomes triggered by an external event and rears its monstrous head or when it begins to organically dissipate as described above. In terms of triggers, I'm sure you can think of plenty of times when a loved one acted in a way that wasn't their "normal" self. Most of the time, the monster (which is only a monster because the energy has been locked away for so long and has become twisted and distorted) will severely overreact to a situation and then retreat into the shadows again after being fed a good dose of rage or whatever type of energy it needs to sustain itself. A few weeks or several months later it will surface again to either be released or fed – one or the other. It will never stay in the shadows for long, as the psyche is not intended to stay divided long term.

As said before, life simply tries to move through us. It doesn't concern itself with old emotions blocking its extension. Picture life energy as the foundation below the two superficial counterparts of presenting self and suppressed self, seeking to move up and out as your unique essence, spirit, or love. (The iceberg metaphor works with this image: the tip is one's presenting self and the layer just below it is the suppressed self, while the base is one's essence, spirit, or pure life energy trying to emerge) Within the psyche, life wants to bubble up through the tip and extend outward, but bumps up against the suppressed self. Each time life energy bumps into this mass of buried emotion, the process of transformation initiates as the suppressions begin to loosen. The contents of the suppressed self ultimately have to pass through one's conscious awareness in order to be released, but because we don't understand what's happening, we become fearful and abruptly react to stop the process. Typically, whenever suppressed energy loosens and moves a bit, we begin to feel off balance and out of control. Unlike emotional triggers, we can sense this disruption in equilibrium coming on, and therefore interrupt the process at will.

We interrupt the onset of organic transformation through the use of our favorite avoidance strategies. In chapter three we will explore in depth the most common avoidance strategies, but in general, anything that numbs or distracts you from discomfort or boredom (indications of inner change) will

weather, but arises out of the dance between clear skies and dark clouds. The same is true within individuals – harmony is not the absence of heavy emotions and periodic discomfort, but the outcome of embracing all our emotions, knowing that they come and go like the weather.

The divided psyche makes the mistake of identifying internal change and temporary disequilibrium with a lack of harmony. It therefore, suppresses the very life that will bring it into balance. This dynamic – life trying to rise up and clear out debris, only to be shoved underground in an effort to maintain internal "harmony" – results in a submerged battle and divided psyche with a thin layer of superficial harmony spread on top. This mindset keeps the psyche divided until enough courage is mustered to withstand transformation.

Transformation awaits all of us. Life naturally wants to dissolve anything in us that is heavy and fear based, making more room for itself. It is that simple and that objective, but we resist, clinging to our identities as we know them, enduring decades – and sometimes lifetimes – of inner division and turmoil. This division is projected onto the world, where it plays out over and over as conflict and war while we scratch our heads in confusion about why we can't end the madness.

Sanity begins with you and me. It begins with the understanding that organic transformation does not destroy, it liberates. It begins with the knowledge that superficial harmony at the expense of real growth leads to imprisonment. We cannot blame ourselves for not wanting to "rock the boat" with another or within ourselves. As we've seen, our quest for homeostasis is rooted in survival instincts. But it has gone too far when we cling to fragile identities built on preserving superficial harmony.

Getting over the harmony myth – the idea that in order to preserve peace we need to resist change and keep things as they are – involves embracing the idea that sustainable health on every level – within oneself, in relationships, organizations, and socially – requires putting life first, supporting its extension above all else. This reorientation from preservation to extension can, and usually does, get a little messy at first, but as we will see, order and health ultimately emerge.

What does reorienting from preservation to extension mean? It means developing a relationship with life or the spirit within you to the point that you can perceive its will – what it asks of you on a moment by moment basis – and following its lead, regardless of the outcome. We don't do this for religious reasons or even because it's "the right thing to do," we do it because it leads to inner and outer peace. What else is there?

For me, this meant leaving a man who didn't want to be married, despite my desperate need (and socialized belief) to make it work. It meant standing up to the terror-invoking fear that walking away would be a huge mistake for me, my child and for him as well. Yet life would have the union crumble and transform into something different – a co-parenting friendship. In retrospect I see that the relationship ending was so right, and that had I stayed I would still be trying to cultivate health in a place where it was not. This is one example of many, coming from someone who is committed to letting life lead. Following life means we move in the direction that our deepest self wants to go – the direction that allows for maximum life flow. Again, surrendering to life is the only real path to inner peace, but we often experience chaos prior to peace – especially when we resist the change for quite a while. Learning to trust the gentle nudges of life ultimately leads to a graceful blossoming infused with a sense of innocent adventure.

To summarize thus far:

- Most of us enter adulthood with a split psyche resulting from socialization and continued repression of feelings.

- Inner division is sub-consciously prolonged out of a desire to preserve harmony.

- An integrated psyche is a portal of peace and is born out of a transformative process led by life.

Chapter 4
Moving from Socialization
to Essentialization

Moving from over-socialization to essentialization is the path presented in this book. The term essentialization came to me in my sleep as a vision or a dream. I simply saw a written equation that looked like this:

Essentialization: moving toward one's essence.

The implication was that essentialization is the opposite or partial undoing of socialization. The essentialized psyche is integrated, clear and open – a portal of peace.

There are five steps to essentialization:

- Charge

- Alchemy

- Shed

- Embody

- Express

Although these steps are presented in order, they often occur simultaneously and, once initiated, are perfectly executed to fit your psychic landscape.

Once essentialized, we are highly unique, as no one is the same at this level, just as no two snow flakes are the same. We are incredibly fulfilled, bright, and passionate. Our essence flows into the world as light, providing a healing effect for both our immediate environment and the world. Our individual piece of the collective consciousness is whole and healed, and through our demonstrated inner-peace and transparency, we encourage others to take this inevitable journey. One by one the landscape of our collective consciousness shifts until there is a quantum leap toward wholeness: At-one-ment. Finally the outer world begins to reflect the peace that has permeated our individual and collective being.

Transformation

It is human nature to construct an identity that feels acceptable to others, shoving aside intense emotions, trauma and aspects of oneself that are a bit "outside the box." As we have seen, however, there is a price to pay for such a sculpted version of self – we actually lose ourselves in this arrangement.

Picture yourself in all your glory, your essence overflowing into the world. So full of yourself – in a good way – that you never hunger for anything other than what nourishes and supports your existence. This is how we are designed to be, however when we hold on to the identity constructed during childhood well into adulthood, our essence and life force goes from lush and overflowing to a trickle – not near enough to feed us the life energy needed to feel good, much less to share this pure nourishment with the world.

It would not be appropriate to expect children to remain completely open and untainted while growing up, as it's an inherently messy process. Much of the suppression we do as kids is out of pure survival. It takes a lot of energy to grow, and we don't really have the resources necessary to process everything that comes our way *and* sprout up like weeds at the same time. As we've discussed, socialization is normal and necessary, and ending up with a pile of unwanted stuff collected along the way is part of it all.

Lucy for example, was a tomboy. She could not have cared less if she ever wore a dress. She liked playing in the dirt and being active – period. But when she became interested in boys, she found that they were not reciprocating. Lucy discovered in junior high that in order to be "popular" she had to become more girly, so she shoved her active self aside and began to wear what the other girls were wearing and sit around at lunch and giggle rather than run around. There is nothing wrong with this. We know that belonging is a basic need, and during pre-teen and teen years this need is exaggerated. It may even be harmful for Lucy to have continued on her path, as she might have experienced trauma from being teased or other repercussions by not conforming at all. Certain kids do choose not to conform at all, and that is fine for them – however, growing up involves a delicate balance of being oneself and trying to fit in. Lucy will likely reclaim her active self as soon as feels secure in her ability to get along well with her peers.

The problem occurs when we get into adulthood and continue to operate as a fragile person that needs continual defending. Pushing "undesirable" pieces of ourselves aside becomes habitual, a way to continue living life as we know it without interruption (the changes associated with transformation). This is when over-socialization occurs – one's identity becomes more and more constricted until it is a fragile house of cards that requires immense amounts of energy to hold up. This is not who you are. You are resilient and strong and whole and unique. No one is the same as another and trying to hold onto the contrived self into adulthood heads us straight toward addiction, mental instability, and a whole host of self-defeating behaviors. These behaviors are attempts to compensate for a lack of real nourishment (life energy) and to keep the fragile house of cards from collapsing.

Perhaps reintroducing a rite of passage that ushers adolescents into adulthood would initiate the process of bringing us home to ourselves. Many traditional cultures and religions have such rituals built into the fabric of their societies. These rites of passage facilitate the process of partial "undoing"– transformation that leads to shedding the layers accumulated over one's essential self.

Every classic children's movie portrays a dramatic rite of passage as its central theme. The main character – usually a child or animal – gets to be a certain age and must go through a series of events, struggles and challenges in order to claim his or her place in the world. If this rite of passage or universal need to embark on a pilgrimage to reclaim oneself is so basic to healthy human existence why do so many of us miss it? Sadly, our mainstream culture is focused more on constant striving for accumulation than "soul searching" or personal transformation. Growth – sure! As long as it isn't messy or doesn't require us to change much.

Spontaneous Transformation

Just because rites of passage are not a part of mainstream American culture doesn't mean we don't get a chance to rediscover ourselves another way. When I was in my twenties, I worked as an inside sales person in a manufacturing company. It got to work in a beautiful office and communicate with smart, interesting people. I could have potentially stayed with that organization for decades – I know people who have – but I began to feel anxious, like I was suffocating. Something was not right and I had to make a change. In retrospect I realize that life was trying to extend through me, but was blocked. Like the scenario described above, I extended my socialized youth into adulthood without interruption or time to integrate what I had suppressed in order to grow. I became more fragile each year that passed until the age of 27, when I was teetering on an anxiety disorder.

An inner voice told me to move away. I describe the journey in my first book, *Opening to Life*, so I won't go into great detail here, but luckily I listened to that voice and took action. Within weeks of arriving in a totally new setting, my life was turned upside down with the onset of a spiritual awakening. My childhood mind was replaced with something much deeper and more connected. It is from this mind that I have rebuilt my life. I often wonder what life would be like had I ignored the voice inside encouraging me to move. I'm pretty certain that I would have felt stuck and even more anxious. I would have likely resorted to food, alcohol or shopping as a way to make myself feel okay. The longer we ignore the voice that urges change, the more fearful and rigid we become.

The fact is, life offered me a pilgrimage and I took it. Life offers everyone the chance to find themselves, to let go of what holds them back, but conventional wisdom states that it's more responsible to accumulate experience, money and maintain a strong work ethic than to go on an "irresponsible journey" leading nowhere. Not everyone is called to move to a different state, but at some point we are each called to shed our outworn selves in favor of who we really are. But let me guard the free spirited reader against the trap of running away from oneself. My pattern was to stay put, which is why I had to move. If you are someone who feels the urge to move or shake things up when life gets a little boring, perhaps your path is to hunker down and burn through the tendency to flee at the moment transformation begins to takes hold.

Inviting Transformation

If you have not had the opportunity to say "Yes" to a transformative experience to help you shed the layers covering your essence, there are things you can do to invite this experience. It all begins with a conscious choice to cultivate a relationship with your spiritual or essential self. This is the part of you that is unseen, but more real and enduring than anything about you that can be seen. We do this by spending time with this part of ourselves on a daily basis. It doesn't so much matter how you do it, just that you make time each day to still your mind and connect with your spirit. Each time you do so, your spiritual identity gets bigger. Slowly but surely your identity shifts from being the tip of the iceberg (your ego) to the vast, supportive, wise essence that lies beneath.

As your connection to the spiritual essence, or life, within you gets stronger, you will begin to hear and feel its urgings. Not only that, you will start to feel more secure in the part of you that is enduring, so that when you are asked to make changes, you will have something to fall back on other than your fragile ego identity. The key is listening or trusting yourself enough to move forward with what you are feeling moved to do.

Some of you already have a strong spiritual core – an identity rooted in the eternal nature of life rather than the parts of your body and personality that are fleeting. You may even be to the point that you listen to the voice of life and act on its guidance. If so, you may have already embraced transformation as a way of life, committing yourself to fully embodying your essence by being willing to let go of anything blocking your light. But if you don't feel like you are quite there yet, keep reading.

As a practicing psychotherapist, it was important for me to ensure that clients had a strong sense of safety and grounding prior to processing any trauma. The client needed to have a place to come back to when the healing process got messy and overwhelming. Cultivating spiritual grounding as a prerequisite to transformation is very similar. Only when we know that we are not the tip of the iceberg, but the foundation that supports it, can the tip be chipped away, modified, or in some cases even demolished in order for a more authentic tip to emerge. Before having that knowledge, we feel threatened at the prospect of even the smallest change, feeling that our identity is at risk.

If you haven't already set a deliberate intention to expand your identity to include your essential self, I recommend that you do so now. Simply invite your essence to expand into your awareness – welcome the spirit of God to lead your journey into wholeness. You can say it out loud, write it down, or say it in a prayer. Honor yourself and do what feels right to you.

Forced Transformation

If we decline the invitation to spontaneously transform and subsequently neglect to invite transformation, then life is left with no other choice than to force the issue. Forced transformation is life's way of bulldozing through rigid and built up corridors, leaving a crumbled mess in its wake.

Forced transformation comes in many disguises. It can come as an illness, a divorce, a job loss or an affair. It can show up as hitting rock bottom in an addiction, bankruptcy or a debilitating disorder such as anxiety or depression, and the list goes on.

It is impossible to escape transformation completely. In rare cases it can be delayed until death – the ultimate transformation. If extreme denial results in a lifetime of procrastination, life will be accompanied by deep pain and discontentment. While one might think that trading a thousand mini-deaths for one huge death is a way to avoid change, pain and disharmony, it is in fact the ultimate avoidance of life.

If you have found yourself picking up the pieces of a forced transformation, consider yourself blessed, for spirit can now shine through the cracks and lead you to a life fuller than you ever imagined.

Chapter 5
Charge

Charging from within by connecting to your spiritual core each day is the first step to essentialization. The increased spiritual energy you receive initiates the process of essentialization the way the sun's rays melt an ice cube. The energy from your core begins a complex reorganization that sheds all that hinders this core energy from radiating outward. Embodying your spirit and pouring it into the world is a cellular experience. You cannot think your way through transformation, as it is not a brain function. Transformation occurs at a completely different level and only sensing and intuiting your way down this organic path will lead you to your essential self.

Set aside some time each day to connect with your core, the way you would dedicate a certain amount of quality time to connect with your child each day. Meditation is one way to do this, but a mindful walk can be as nourishing as sitting down to meditate. There are also numerous opportunities throughout the day to tune in to yourself and connect to the spirit that is in and all around you. Conscious breathing is the super highway to one's spiritual core. This can be done at any time. As you follow your breath to your abdomen and out again, you strengthen the connection to your eternal self.

It is important to be flexible about how you connect with your higher self. You are your ultimate teacher. Do what feels right to you, for whatever way you connect to this calm source of energy and inner peace is fine.

Developing the ability to quiet your mind is also supremely important. Even though you've likely heard it a million times, many do not realize the significance of mental discipline. Spiritual or life energy is contained in every cell of your being, and swimming in circles in your head with the same thoughts over and over prevents you from hearing and feeling this sacred presence.

Picture yourself on a train headed to a meeting. You are riding through Montana where the trees are lush and natural beauty is abundant. You happen to be hyper-focused on your laptop trying to get some things done. When you arrive, the person who picks you up says, "Can you believe the spectacular view from the train?" All of a sudden you realize that you completely forgot to notice. The same is true when we constantly think – excessive attention on our thoughts distracts us from the abundant energy, information and inspiration contained in the life energy in and around us.

Therefore, while flexibility in your spiritual practice is important, it is vital to somehow incorporate mental stillness and conscious breathing into each day. Meditation is a natural way to accomplish both these things, but I'm afraid that so many people already beat themselves up for not having a regular meditation practice that it becomes a source of guilt. Simply do what you can. If you can spend one minute in the shower paying attention to your breath instead of your thoughts, go for it. If you can spend another minute in your car on the way to work appreciating the sky and trees, great! Just do what you can, and you will find that the more you plug into this source of amazingly supportive and nourishing energy, the more you will want to, and the easier it will be. I begin to crave spiritual nourishment when I've been particularly busy and will often step away for a moment to steal a kiss with God. The nourishment we seek is closer than your next breath. It often helps to start by taking a deep breath and thinking to yourself, *it's even closer;* you will then sense a charge of energy rush into your body, making you new again.

Strengthen Your Foundation

As mentioned above, there is another reason that charging is the place to start when choosing the path of essentialization. In addition to initiating transformation, developing a strong connection to your spiritual core allows your identity to expand from the fragile presenting self to the part of you that is eternal and completely safe from external changes.

This is a supremely important step toward essentialization. Growth cannot occur without attachment. We have to be able to at least hold on to a rope while jumping off the cliff into the unknown. The connection to your essence is your rope. Each time you plug in to your essence and remain still long enough for spiritual energy to begin to flow upward, your essence expands as does your connection to it. Ultimately your essence inhabits your entire being – not only resting at the surface of your skin, but emanating beyond it the way a light shines beyond a light bulb.

As you will see in the next chapter, we are required to participate in the essentialization process. The ego survives because it is fed, and at a point, we need to stop feeding it. The only way to endure the fear and discomfort of letting go of your false self is to develop a connection to something greater – your essential self. This occurs much in the way that a teenager needs a strong attachment to his or her peers in order to release a layer of parental attachment that was necessary for early childhood development, but hinders emerging adulthood.

Let Life Lead

The journey from the presenting self to the essentialized self is a bit like using your senses to walk through your house in the dark. As I said before, this is not a mental journey, nor can it be planned. As you become increasingly charged with life, however, it will begin to guide you in very practical, but subtle ways. It will also begin presenting whatever needs to be released in the shadows of your being in a way that is both manageable and systematic. Remember the model of the socialized psyche.

You have your presenting self or ego identity and right below it is your suppressed self – everything you've experienced up to now that's been too overwhelming or painful to process. Beneath the presenting self and the suppressed self is a combination of your unique essence and universal life energy that seeks to flow through and beyond you.

As the connection to your essence is strengthened, life's natural tendency to flow upward is supported. As life bubbles up, the unseen contents of your shadows begin to loosen-up and enter your awareness. The shadows contain messages from your higher self that you've ignored; the feelings of pain and loss you've shoved aside; the fear of failure associated with living big… All of it, little by little, floats into your awareness to be processed and released. This work has to be done eventually, and it's too big of a job to put off until we're too tired to do it.

This is why we're often reminded that things get worse before they get better – or messier before getting cleaner. This is also why so many of us habitually distract ourselves from what we know we need to do – we intuitively know that facing ourselves involves a good spring cleaning.

However, if you can tolerate the spring cleaning, the gifts of life flowing through are tremendous – inspiration, hope and guidance are among them. The guidance you receive can sometimes seem silly, but can also illicit a strong fear of change. Anything, such as, "Stop drinking soda," or "Say what's on your mind…" may pop into your head as life begins to direct you. At this stage it is important to keep listening – even if you are not yet ready to act on the guidance.

From the time of my spiritual awakening, I was given guidance to periodically fast. It took me over a decade to heed this particular piece of guidance, and although I tried to ignore it, the guidance persisted year after year, patiently waiting for me to listen.

My point is that you may not be ready to act on each bit of intuition you receive, but if you keep listening, it will keep talking and that is what's most important. When you follow the voice of life, you'll experience unmistakable feelings of inner peace. It is not necessary, or even productive, to do everything at once to feel this peace, only to be on the path, continue listening and make small changes along the way. In my case, I took baby steps by eliminating toxins from my diet and eating healthy foods until I felt prepared to integrate periodic fasting into my routine.

Guidance from your essential self, and the universal spiritual energy within, is always customized for you – perfectly tailored in fact. That is why advice from experts must resonate with your internal wisdom in order for it to work. For example, not all health and fitness programs apply to everyone because each approach is ultimately geared toward the person who created it. You may need something entirely different to balance your body and bring it into perfect health. This is true for everything from financial investments to the way you communicate with others. Sure, there is a lot to be learned from experts, but the real expert on you is you!

Following your own guidance takes some getting used to particularly if you are in the habit of constantly looking outside yourself for answers. But once you learn to trust your intuition, you will find that every aspect of life becomes infinitely easier. Here are some tips.

- Pay attention to your hunches.

- Never dismiss a gut feeling.

- Intuitive insights come in a flash – learn the difference between circular thinking and an inspired flash of insight.

- Dreams contain the truth of your psyche – always look beneath the surface of the content in your dreams to the underlying themes.

- If something doesn't feel right it's not.

- Hearing voices doesn't always mean you're crazy – it is a valid way that life communicates with us and is called clairaudience.

- Until you feel complete conviction, don't share you're intuition with others. Once you know it to be true, you won't be as easily swayed by those seeking to "help" with contrary advice.

It's a mistake to ask other people to validate your intuition or guidance. This level of information often flies in the face of conventional wisdom, leading people to think that you are being "irrational." The path of essentialization is not for those who desperately need approval. It is for people who are willing to do what they feel is right despite what others think.

Finally, we all make mistakes when learning to trust our own guidance. It's like learning to ride a bike, but once you get the hang of it, it's smooth sailing. Until then it feels a little frightening and you'll probably fall a couple of times before mastering this balancing act.

Communicating with Your Essence Exercise

Your essence continuously communicates with you about what it needs to expand and extend through you. Listening and following it is your only job. Take a moment to visit with your essence. Breathe deeply as your awareness sinks below the surface of your mind. With each breath, go deeper and deeper. Once you feel still inside, ask your essence: "What do you need me to do now?" Wait for the answer. You may get a feeling or thought, see a picture or hear words. If you do not get a sense of your next step, know that it will come to you in your next moment of silence – perhaps in a dream or in the shower. Thank your essence for communicating with you and make a promise that you will always listen.

There are two major points to remember about charging. The first is that developing a strong relationship with your essential self builds the foundation necessary to follow the voice of life, which may direct you to make changes in order to embody more of the real you.

Lucky for us, life never stops trying to extend through us and beyond us. Just like water flowing down a stream would never simply stop if it encountered a pile of rocks in its path, it continues to flow forth modifying the landscape with its force. And the way the same river chisels through a mountain until it becomes a canyon, this alchemic process occurs naturally and organically – our only job is to stop delaying our own evolution by interrupting it.

According to Webster, Alchemy is defined as the process of transmuting a common substance, usually of little value, into a substance of great value. In this case,

Alchemy transmutes lower, heavy repressed energy into lighter energy that can be released, thereby making more room for pure life-force to flow through. Over-socialization brings with it an inner landscape full of debris, and although everyone's internal pile of debris looks different, the socialized psyche always has the same agenda: to preserve the presenting self by keeping the suppressed buried. The cost of continuing to shove down undesirable emotions, personality traits and trauma in order to preserve what one believes to be his identity is unbelievable: constricted life flow, a complete lack of inner peace, and ongoing conflict in the world.

Each of us is faced with two options: dedicate each moment to continually stopping the flow of life to avoid the unknown, or become witness to our own graceful transformation.

Warrior Strength

Anyone who has not already adopted transformation as a way of life knows deep down that a shift needs to happen – that they need to do something: Make a change, stand up for themselves, take a risk, or perhaps stop avoiding what needs to be done in order to grow. But let's not deny the white elephant in the room – transformation invokes terror. What always comes to mind is the caterpillar climbing up a tree in order to spin a chrysalis. If the caterpillar had any idea that it was about to completely dissolve prior to becoming a butterfly it would stay on the ground and munch on grass until dying of obesity or old age. Luckily, it doesn't know, so it follows its instincts, climbs up a tree, spins a chrysalis and emerges as a vibrant butterfly. All is well and right in caterpillar land. But, we have conscious awareness that alerts us that we're about to dissolve – our ego anyway – and hey, it's frightening!

Because, like a caterpillar, we change at a cellular level when we dedicate ourselves to the greater good and commit to releasing anything that would block our light, only the strength of a warrior will allow us to push through the fear. We are given this strength by virtue of shifting our identities from the tip of the iceberg to the base (from ego to essence). At a point, we know that not even death can destroy us, and it is this type of courage that makes true transformation possible.

Avoidance Strategies

Interrupting transformation through the use of avoidance strategies is equivalent to the caterpillar staying on the ground and eating grass. *Why rock the boat? It's comfortable, we're not starving…* The truth is that accepting mediocrity as a way of life is no life at all. We are destined for more and trying to be content with less never works.

A few words about the nature of avoidance strategies: As we know, anything buried below conscious awareness is projected outward and then perceived as coming from the outside and completely separate from ourselves. This is true for our suppressed emotions, as well as our light. Avoidance strategies may help us maintain equilibrium and dodge the discomfort associated with emotional processing, but continuing to repress old emotional residue involves denying one's essence and light. Being buried, our light is projected onto various things in our environment: Other people, food, perhaps a substance, things like clothes, cars and toys, power, money. The list goes on. Seeing the energy (our own spirit) we so desperately crave in the object it's projected onto, we chase it and eventually marry it, consume it, buy it or earn it. The energy we get from consuming the object of desire is like a drop in the ocean. It gives only an instant of comfort before the chase is back on. And again, again, and again – the chase for ourselves is potentially endless. In truth, there is only one way to fill ourselves up with the nourishment we crave – life energy – and that is to embody and express it. Projection is an unending game of seek and find, as we never find what we are seeking. This is the dynamic that fuels avoidance strategies: Our light begins to bubble up and dissipate the layers of congestion that fog and conceal it, we become uncomfortable and rather than embrace the discomfort, we distract ourselves by shining our light outward and then desperately moving toward it, and eventually stuffing ourselves with it, in the hopes that it will fill us up. The biggest tragedy of all is that the attempt to capture our essence in an external object creates another layer of fog on top of our essence.

There are as many avoidance strategies as there are people on the planet, but listed below are some of the most common ways that we interrupt our own evolution.

Alcohol Abuse

Excessive alcohol consumption is an attempt to feel one's spirit – which is why some drinks are called "spirits." Alcohol gives a high similar to the exhilaration that comes from being high on life, only it is short lived and often destructive. People who crave this type of high need to be willing to sit through some boredom and tension long enough to burn through whatever is blocking their own spirit. Addicts are some of the most spirited people around and they deeply crave the intensity that comes from channeling one's spirit at a high velocity. Any lull in this intensity can drive such a spirited person to drink. The answer however, is in the lull not the drink.

Angry Outbursts

Anger is a normal emotion that arises when something is wrong. It is only unhealthy when it becomes a pattern or habitual way of controlling one's environment and inner feelings. When we become out of control and have outbursts that are inappropriate and out of proportion to the situation, we are using anger to aggressively stop our own feelings from surfacing. The feelings we defend against range from anxiety to shame or sadness. The myth is that the outburst is a justified reaction to the person or situation that "caused" the anger. Each time an uncontrollable outburst occurs, some of the violent energy is suppressed on top of whatever was there to begin with. To stop this pattern, the anger must be felt without having an outburst. This way the anger sitting on top of the other feelings can dissipate, allowing the deeper ones to surface. This is when real progress toward integration occurs.

Anorexia

Anorexia is a complex and potentially life-threatening illness that cannot be sufficiently addressed in this context. However, in terms of an avoidance strategy, exerting any type of extreme control over one's diet and body gives the illusion of having control over one's inner world and any chaos in the outer world. Anorexia is the ultimate rejection of one's feelings, starting with the physical sensation of hunger. Getting into treatment and learning to safely feel what's happening inside regardless of outer circumstances is an important step toward overcoming this dangerous pattern.

Approval Seeking

Excessive need for approval indicates that one is cut off from the voice within that offers both clear direction and the knowledge that self-worth lies deeper than outward appearances. While this pattern often arises from childhood circumstances, it can only be transformed in the present. Challenging oneself to make autonomous decisions prior to seeking feedback from others is a good place to start. Getting some distance from overly controlling people is also essential. Finally, cultivating a bit of a rebellious spirit goes a long way. Trust yourself!

Bulimia

Also complex and dangerous, the ritual of bulimia involves stuffing oneself (one's feelings) in a frenzied, animalistic fashion and then purging to get it all out. This is an indirect attempt to clear one's feelings. As with all avoidance strategies, the strategy becomes an issue in itself, simply adding to the reservoir of suppressed emotional energy. Clients struggling with bulimia that I've worked with have made huge strides in terms of healing when they honor their feelings and express them directly to others rather than stuff them. In addition to direct emotional expression, the person will have to resist the intense desire to purge regardless of how much has been consumed. Without the release valve, the payoff of overeating will diminish and inner peace will eventually emerge.

Complaining

Chronic complaining takes one out of the present moment and into a world of distraction and negativity. Focusing attention on what's "wrong" in the outer world is a way of avoiding one's inner world through the use of deflection. Each complaint provides just enough heavy energy (not as heavy as gossip) to sit on top of the suppressed self and the life underneath it that would otherwise flow through. Complaining is simply a habit of distorting life flow that can be changed through commitment and mindful awareness.

Control

Attempting to control another is a common way that people try to avoid internal anxiety or repressed feelings, and although it is impossible to control people or events, they can often be manipulated or delayed, which reinforces the controlling behavior. Control of any kind is the opposite of surrender and an ineffective attempt to avoid uncomfortable emotions that are trying to surface. Once the identity shifts to one's essential nature, surrender replaces control and we learn to "go with the flow."

Conflict Avoidance

Avoiding conflict is a pattern often learned in childhood when the price of conflict is too high. When someone gets pounced every time a conflict arises, the natural outcome is to avoid it all together. It is terrifying for a person with this type of pattern to embrace healthy conflict, as any level of discord brings up old trauma. Not only does the avoider not trust others, he or she does not trust themselves due to not having had the opportunity to develop the skill to express intense emotions. Therefore, avoiding conflict is really avoiding one's feelings and the life energy contained in the feelings. Learning diplomacy and the ability to assertively express oneself is the way out of this life constricting pattern.

Drug Abuse

Abusing either illegal or prescription drugs is an attempt to numb out and distract oneself from reality. In addition to avoiding personal growth, all addictions add another layer of dysfunction which eventually will need to be addressed. Asking what feeling the drug provides is a way to find out what needs to be cultivated within. Some drugs are calming while others are stimulating. The abuse of calming drugs indicates a need for grounding and routine, as well as the need to develop coping skills to deal with everyday life so that "checking-out" is not longer required. Abusing stimulants indicates a craving for more spiritual energy, in which case it is essential to stop using in order to burn off any physical and emotional residue blocking the flow of life.

Electronic Addiction

Electronic addiction is the compulsive need to be plugged into or constantly connected to electronic devices. Cell phones, MP3 players, computers, televisions and video games all fall into this category. Tuning into an electronic device deceives one into thinking they are connected, when really they are becoming increasingly disconnected from their internal source of energy. This addiction is on the rise with a new generation that has grown up being "wired" to such devices. Productivity and personal growth are replaced with distraction and preoccupation. These devices offer a false sense of security and invoke anxiety when not available. Weaning one's self from these devices and changing one's thoughts is necessary to release the compulsive need to be externally connected, allowing a healthy connection within to develop.

Emotional Eating

Eating for reasons other than hunger is an unconscious attempt to "stuff" heavy emotional residue that is trying to come to the surface and be released. The concrete energy of extra food adds to the lower vibration of suppressed energy within oneself. The combination of these energies creates an entity in itself that acts like a wild animal. This untamed energy mass must be fed regularly in order to survive. That is why emotional eating is such a difficult habit to break – stopping this behavior results in acute discomfort as the heavy energy breaks up and releases from the body. One's center of discipline or will (located at the solar plexus or abdomen) needs to be strengthened through restraint. After only several times of not giving in to the impulse to over-eat, spiritual energy can flow more freely and become a more refined source of energy. In no time at all, cravings for food will only occur in response to physical hunger.

Giving too Much

Over-giving can be defined as *doing for others at the expense of oneself.* This behavior indicates low self-worth, and is often supported by an unconscious belief that one is inherently unlovable. Feeling unlovable, the over-giver tries to earn adoration. Cultivating unconditional regard for oneself is the first step to breaking this depleting habit, and comes naturally from deepening one's spiritual connection – the internal source of energy and self-worth. In truth, one's biggest gift to others is being happy and fulfilled from within. Over-givers pour vital energy that should be used for self-care and passionate self-expression onto others in the hopes that it will come back and fulfill the giver's needs. It never does, and therefore becomes fuel for resentment. Offering one's time, energy and attention out of inspiration rather than obligation is the key to conscious giving. Inspiration translates to "in-spirit," which means you are full of spiritual energy to the point of it moving through your heart center before extending outward. This is the only type of giving that nourishes both the giver and receiver.

Guilt and Shame

Guilt and shame are the lowest vibrating emotions. They are not only heavy, but sticky – literally keeping one stuck in the same toxic behaviors that caused the guilt and shame in the first place. Like all other pockets of suppressed energy, guilt and shame need to be fed regularly in order to sustain. Each new guilt or shame producing episode feeds this emotional mass, keeping it alive. In order to transform the self-defeating behaviors that perpetuate these sticky emotions, one must refuse to wallow in their resulting guilt and shame. Only then will these heavy emotions dissipate. It is natural to feel remorse after doing something wrong or hurtful, but habitual guilt and shame is an addiction in itself and should be treated as such.

Judging

Judging others and the surrounding world is a habit that keeps one in his or her head, within rigid boxes that provide an illusion of security and control. This mental habit stems from a deep insecurity as a result of not knowing one's eternal self. Focusing on another's shortcomings becomes a way to avoid one's own. Clinging to judgments replaces authentic perception and passionate living. In addition to carefully monitoring and replacing judgmental thoughts as they arise, cultivating a relationship with one's spiritual essence will loosen the grip of meaningless judgments that simply imprison the judger.

Love Addiction

Nothing is more intoxicating than new love. But this "high" inevitably transforms into something deeper and more comfortable. Maturing love also has the effect of exposing one's wounds. With love addiction, the person unconsciously avoids these hot spots by running at the first sign of activation. Rather than burn through one's "issues," the love addict flees, replacing his or her object of affection with someone new. Projecting one's source onto another becomes a habitual substitute for feeling the high of one's own spirit moving through the body. Love addiction can also be present in a long-term relationship. In this case, the intensity of new love is generated by a destructive cycle of "break-up to make-up." The only way to transform the habit of chasing one's projected spirit is to sit on the craving when it comes up rather than act it out. For example, by refusing to pursue someone new or initiate a fight with an existing partner, the behavior pattern is burned off and the real high of spiritual energy can be enjoyed in the context of a healthy relationship. For more information on love addiction, I recommend the book *Facing Love Addiction* by Pia Mellody.

Nitpicking

Picking at others is a habit that indicates a need for control and is also a way of getting attention and energy – pick by pick. Nitpicking may stem from abandonment issues and the fear that if one doesn't pull people in their direction, they may not stay. Additionally, this behavior pattern is another attempt to control external circumstances as a way to overcompensate for an internal world that feels out of control. Once the criticism is stopped, one's own messy feelings will surface. The nitpicker knows this instinctively and therefore clings to the behavior as if it were a lifeline. Feeling whatever comes up, rather than avoiding it by focusing on others, is the first step to wholeness. The rest involves the deliberate and conscious release of a bad (and annoying) habit.

Obsessive Thinking/Worrying

Running in circles in one's mind has the effect of creating and then feeding mental patterns that end up with a life of their own. These mental monsters distract oneself from reality and the essential self where creative thoughts are born. Excessive mental attention causes one to be "in the clouds" and have a lack of grounding – the exact conditions for worry and anxiety to flourish. A deepening of the relationship with one's ground of being – spiritual core – is required in order to transfer attention from disembodied thoughts to innate wisdom. Living in one's head is a defense mechanism that involves making up reality instead of experiencing it, thereby disconnecting the thinker from him or herself. As with all avoidance strategies, turning within and feeling what's really there, despite the discomfort, helps to shift from fantasy to reality. Putting attention on the toes or doing a progressive relaxation helps bring one's energy and attention back into the body.

Over Socializing

Anything done to excess is a distraction from one's growth. Spending too much time with others is one way to avoid the "still small voice" within that continually urges us toward behaviors that support our evolution. Asking oneself, "Is there something else I need to be doing right now?" is a good way to find out if spending time with others has become a substitute for *Right Action.*

Perfectionism

Perfectionism is a habit of self-rejection. It is conditional self-love. *"Everything will be okay when..."* is the mantra of this avoidance strategy. The list of perfect circumstances one could wait for in order to feel at peace is endless, and the habit of perfectionism is such that even when the desired circumstances arrive, happiness and inner peace are once again denied as another set of expectations emerge. Perfectionism is a way to push aside the life force that is trying to come to the surface. With life force comes all that is buried – old emotions and rejected aspects of oneself, as well as one's gifts and hidden passions. A gradual awareness of self – and ultimately acceptance of the perfect essence that permeates our imperfect forms is the only remedy for the habit of perfection seeking. Gently shifting one's attention from abstract perfectionist ideals to whatever sensations and feelings are present in the body brings one back to reality, while loosening the power of the mental concepts that keep one stuck. The irony is that when the flow of life energy is supported by bringing awareness to sensations in the body, it can do its job of dissolving everything that is *not* authentic and real. Only then can the "ideal" version of oneself emerge.

Power Struggles

Power struggles are an attempt to get love, validation or attention from another. They commonly occur in the second stage of an intimate relationship, after the honeymoon stage where love is given freely. Power struggles are symptomatic of a divided psyche, in which a person's access to his own spiritual power is blocked by the suppressed self. Because spiritual power can't rise up naturally, it is projected onto another person and then chased down through a conflict or argument. The power and love we seek can never be captured, but can only be received from within. There is only one way out of this peace destroying pattern and that is to stop your part of the power struggle dynamic and feel the burn of inner transformation. The burn makes more room for life, love, power. When we are full of life it can flow freely toward others, thereby eliminating the need to fight over this precious resource.

Procrastination

Delaying what needs to be done is one of the most direct ways the light of spiritual energy is diverted from its path of internal transformation and self-expression. Procrastination is a frustrating pattern for those who struggle with it, as this behavior tends to produce guilt. Guilt exaggerates the pattern of procrastination by making it a terrible character defect in the mind of the procrastinator. Breaking free of this self-defeating behavior requires that the guilt be released first. When one does not allow himself to feel excessively "bad" after a bout of procrastination, the top layer of the pattern will dissolve, making the behavior itself easier to transcend with right action. Without the guilt, one can gently move in the direction of what needs to be done. As life begins to flow again, the pattern of procrastination slowly disappears.

Sex Addiction

Buried deep in the individual consciousness of many, and the collective consciousness of society, is repressed sexual energy. The dark shadow of repressed sexual energy serves as a magnet to those who have not taken the time to discipline and refine their own sexual impulses. In order to integrate any kind of repression, we need to allow whatever is buried to come to the surface and pass through awareness without feeding it unconsciously or compulsively. This is challenging, because as it releases, sexual sensations are felt in the body. In order to release repressed sexual energy, one must be able to feel sexual without acting out in a sexual manner. Acting on addictive sexual impulses only feeds this monster, making it bigger, more powerful, and hungry. Once the repressed energy is successfully released, (often after many times of allowing oneself to feel aroused without giving into sexual urges) this primal desire can be appreciated and enjoyed without compulsivity.

Shopping Excessively

Consumption is a necessary part of life, as everyone needs food, shelter and clothing to survive, but consuming to fill a void is the unconscious pursuit of self. Spiritual energy, or the essence of oneself, can only be found within. However, the essence of a great many individuals is buried underneath a layer of emotional congestion, which creates feelings of desperation and hunger. Anything buried or suppressed is projected onto things and people outside oneself then subsequently chased. It follows that compulsive shopping is the act of projecting one's own life energy onto the object of desire and then thinking the only way to get energized and inspired is to buy it. Of course, one gets only a short burst of energy from anything outside oneself, and so the chase is never ending. Not giving in to the urge to chase oneself through compulsive shopping is the only way to pull back one's projection and ultimately connect directly to the real source of energy within.

Working too Much

Workaholism, like any other compulsive behavior, is designed to distract one from what is really important. Family, health, and quality of life suffer while running on the treadmill of unending work. Another avoidance of self – working too much teaches the person the irrational belief that if work is neglected everything will fall to pieces. This compulsive behavior can only be transcended by choosing to live consciously, according to one's core values. This can be a challenging behavior to overcome, as "working hard" is not taboo in society, and can even be viewed as honorable. Seeing it for what it is – a compulsive distraction from one's authentic self and values – is the first step to mindfully moving beyond it. The moment one tunes in to his or her inner self, the voice of life will speak about what is really important.

Victimization

Nearly everyone succumbs to feeling like a victim at times, which makes this mental and emotional avoidance strategy a pervasive part of the individual and collective psyche. Socialization creates an external orientation – the tendency to look outside one self for the reasons things go wrong. This pattern undermines the integration of one's psyche by placing attention and energy in the wrong place. Taking total responsibility for one's internal state is the only way to transcend this avoidance strategy. External situations cannot be controlled, but the way one responds to them can. Learning to stay expanded and open within, despite what is going on in the outer world, allows nourishing life energy to flow no matter what. Inner peace is a byproduct of energy flow, so in reality, one can experience inner peace regardless of external circumstances.

Avoidance strategies can become invoked any time you feel restless, bored or unsteady. It is also common to have overlapping patterns, such as seeing oneself as a victim and compulsive shopping. This overlap creates an intertwined web of self-defeating dynamics. My point in illuminating these behaviors is to illustrate how many ways we can stuff, avoid, distort, and inhibit the flow of life. We do this unconsciously from the ego, or small "I" that feels the need to defend itself against its own death. The death of the small "I" is inevitable, however, and the pain is short lived. Coming to terms with this fact and moving forward as a conscious participant in our own evolution leads to inner peace.

As you can see, avoidance strategies are attempts to gain control. As life energy rises in order to extend through us, any emotional and physical debris loosens and enters our awareness. Panicked, we compulsively turn to a familiar habit and pour our energy in that direction. What happens next is a combination of forces that work together to maintain equilibrium and preserve the split psyche for a while longer. Just to review the dynamic of the split psyche:

1. We suppress (and subsequently repress) intense emotions and parts of ourselves that are uncomfortable in order to get them out of awareness.

2. Because the repressed energy has to go somewhere, it is then projected onto various people, objects, rituals or substances.

3. We then proceed to chase or consume the people, objects or substances that carry projected pieces of ourselves as an unconscious attempt to recapture the energy we're losing in the projections.

4. The compulsive pursuit or consumption of the person, object, activity or substance has the effect of re-pressing the contents of the buried psyche back out of awareness, as well shoving down the spiritual energy that is naturally trying to rise up and extend into the world. When the chase is over, we have successfully stuffed fresh, life energy once again in favor of heavy, recycled energy, thereby keeping us blocked and divided.

This unconscious ritual preserves the divided inner landscape for a while – a few days or weeks – and relief is experienced for a time, and then it happens all over again. In reality, this dynamic prevents the short term discomfort associated with internal cleansing and integration, while cutting us off from the life energy we so desperately crave and are meant to channel abundantly. The craving for life only perpetuates the cycle of looking for our essence where it doesn't exist.

At some level we feel very conflicted inside each time we engage in an avoidance strategy, vowing to change and overcome the "bad habit." Yet the next time life starts to rise up and loosen the congestion, we find ourselves compulsively headed toward these behaviors the way a starving wild animal devours its prey. By avoiding the discomfort associated with cravings, we really avoid life, our essential selves, and ultimately inner peace.

The mistake most of us make is to over-focus on the "bad" behavior, forgetting the primary source of the problem. We join a diet program to get a hold of our emotional eating. We enter therapy to stop our angry outbursts. We get sober only to begin over-spending. The behavior certainly needs to be addressed and stopped, but the cause of dysfunction ultimately comes from trying to avoid transformation. Therefore rooting one's motivation in "quitting" the behavior alone doesn't provide enough fuel for sustainable change. Motivation infused with power comes from a soul desire to let our light shine, to free our spirits, and to heal ourselves and the world -- despite the discomfort that occurs as we allow life's fire to mold us into strong vessels for its expression. The will of life combined with your small will can move mountains, however your small will alone can move nothing.

Enter the Fire

As portals of peace, we are now called to enter alchemic transformation - to allow the fire of life to burn off all that is blocking it and mold us into a strong vessel with no leaks or cracks. Each time we avoid life, we have another opportunity to choose again, and once we do, we begin to really live – to move closer to our essence instead of running from it. It's important to remember that it doesn't matter how far along you are or how far you think you have to go to reach essentialization, nor does it matter how old you are when you begin, only that you are moving. By honoring life and putting it in charge, you receive all the gifts it leaves in its wake: inner peace, inspiration and a sense of purpose. From life's perspective, there is no time, it only longs to be received and extended. Any time that we support this process, we are fed and life continues.

Essentialization is the result of burning off everything blocking your light while simultaneously allowing your essence to penetrate your cells and make you bright with life. As we move according to the dictates of life, we know that things are bound to get messy. The fear of transformation and change is always bigger than the real thing however. The process of alchemy is straightforward and only happens in the present. It is not intellectual, it is instinctual. When we deal only with what's in front of us we are perfectly guided to the center of ourselves. It's as if you are walking a labyrinth – you walk mindfully to your core, taking small turns along the way. Anything other than moment by moment direction can cause us to feel overwhelmed and fearful. If you are the praying kind, try this prayer:

> *Dear God, I commit my life to you that I might be a bright light in this world and experience deep inner peace that only comes from you. My core desire is to demonstrate peace rather than project division. Please guide me gently and surely so that I do not become overwhelmed. Thank you for the strength and conviction to embrace my essence and share it with the world.*

If you are not comfortable with prayer, simply talk to the life within you and commit to allowing it to extend forth as is naturally intended. Ask that it be gentle in its extension so that you don't get overwhelmed. Whether you are religious or not, life is life – it is all knowing, and is the essence of who you are. It will hear you and respond to you, always.

Tolerating Tension

In the alchemy phase of essentialization, the first step is to observe your own avoidance strategies. What are your self-defeating patterns? Most of us have several – one or two ways we manipulate energy through relationships, negative thought patterns that we milk on a regular basis, as well as a substance, person or object that we compulsively chase or use to distract ourselves when feelings of discomfort and disequilibrium occur.

Burning off the blocks to life and the familiar grooves that have become your avoidance strategies requires the ability to tolerate tension. With this bigger picture in mind, you now have the will and conviction needed to take the next step. Your only job during the alchemy phase is to replace impulsive avoidance strategies with mindful behavior. This is not to say that you never eat ice cream, or tell your spouse when you're annoyed, or shop for clothes. It means that when you are tempted to do so as an unconscious or compulsive reaction to discomfort in your body, you wait until the pressing urge passes. Simply observe your mind trying to lead you in that direction and your body wanting to follow. Feel the burning sensation in your belly as the fire of life dissolves any heavy energy living in the shadows.

Take, for example, an impulse to fight with your mate. In this case, everything in you will want to make a nasty comment. To support alchemy and move toward essentialization, you will resist the urge to fight, leave the room and breathe. You may go for a walk, write in your journal, or clean the house. The tension you feel could dissipate in a few minutes or it might last a few days. Try to delay your reaction for at least a few minutes. If you eventually give in and snap, congratulate yourself on delaying your reaction and being in the tension for a short time. Each moment of tension means that a tiny pocket of suppressed energy has been freed.

GUILT ALERT: Do not let yourself fall into guilt. There is no room for perfectionism as you move toward essentialization. As we've discussed, guilt is like glue, it keeps you stuck. It is one of the heaviest, stickiest emotions, and also one of the slickest avoidance strategies. We think we are being noble when we feel guilty – like we are repenting. True repenting involves taking responsibility for your behavior, making it right when possible, and then promptly forgiving yourself – in other words getting back on track. Guilt will divert you from your path like nothing else.

That said, if someone else is affected by your avoidance strategy, it's important that you recognize that within yourself and with him or her. In the end "Sorry is as sorry does," and right action is required. Rest assured that, despite normal set backs, each time you feel the alchemic fire burning through internal blocks; you're making more room for pure life energy to penetrate your cells. This means that the next time you feel the urge to engage in an avoidance strategy you will be more empowered to withstand the temptation. Change and growth don't move in a straight upward line, rather we zigzag while slowly moving toward overall health. Try not to feel defeated by setbacks. We know that transformation is organic and physical in nature, and therefore takes time, just like a baby takes time to gestate in the womb. The new you is coming forth, one choice at a time. Stick with it and one day you will experience a peace deeper than you've ever imagined, and you will know that you've become a bright light in a world that desperately needs it.

A little more needs to be said on the organic nature of transformation. We live in an immediate gratification society. We have very little tolerance for the time in between cause and effect. The truth is that as long as we inhabit a human body, there will be a delay. While in this delay, it is common to feel that no progress is being made. Sometimes we feel bored, like we are *dying* to shake things up a bit. Part of becoming educated on the process of transformation is being aware of this delay and how you respond to it. I find myself wanting to go shopping when the life inside me seems to be standing still. It's as if I think I can buy a new me… We can't buy a new version of ourselves, or birth one instantly by "hooking up" with someone, or unleash our spirit by drinking too many cocktails. Getting comfortable with feeling nothing inside is as important as being comfortable with tension.

This is an aspect of faith – knowing that doing the right thing will lead to inner freedom, peace, and being high on life – literally. There's no substitute for personal experience, however, so you will need to discover this for yourself. The inevitable delay between right action and embodying your spirit is part of real transformation. It's the same principle as when you go on a diet. You eat right for a day or two, and it isn't until a few days later that that results show up on the scale. The same is true for healing and essentialization – in the physical world there will always be a delay. The delay does get shorter as we get clearer however.

It is possible to ease feelings of tension and boredom with physical activity. Running, yoga, dancing, cleaning, gardening, walking – almost anything physical will shake off tension and increase the velocity of energy flowing through your body, helping you to feel content and at ease in your own skin. Other activities can make you feel more comfortable too – only you know what constitutes healthy self-care versus what is an avoidance strategy.

One client expressed surprise when I suggested she comfort herself during a difficult time by playing the piano, praying for support, or having a nice meal. "I thought I was just supposed to sit in the tension!" She exclaimed. There are times when the only thing we can do is be with our tension – these are times when you feel completely overwhelmed and cannot think to do anything but sit with the discomfort. But anytime you can do something that connects you to your source and helps you feel more at peace, by all means do so.

The Alchemy phase of essentialization is the most difficult initially. However, once you get a feel for how to burn off self-defeating patterns and emotional congestion, regular transformation becomes a part of life. It's like cleaning your house. If you let junk pile up for twenty years, the initial cleaning is going to be pretty difficult, but once it's clean, it's much easier to keep it that way by keeping things tidy (making intuitive decisions as you go to avoid heavy karma and internal congestion later) while doing spring cleanings as needed (going a little deeper when life calls on you to make changes.)

Emotional versus
Physical Congestion

Defense mechanisms, such as suppression and repression, come to our rescue when we are overwhelmed with emotion. They help us maintain our equilibrium or balance, and are necessary protectors of our psyche. They can, however, become habitual, leaning us too heavily toward equilibrium even when we are in need of a good release. Continuous suppression and repression of uncomfortable feelings leads to emotional congestion. This heavy, unprocessed energy clogs our system and prevents us from feeling fully alive. And as we've discussed, anything suppressed leads to projection – seeing the contents of your psyche in others and reacting to the perception as if it is solely coming from outside yourself.

Physical congestion, on the other hand, is the result of ingesting food, substances, or toxins in excess of what your body is able to process. This congestion also builds up over time if we do not intentionally release it or prevent build-up in the first place.

Over-consuming food or alcohol is a common avoidance strategy. We unconsciously engage in compulsive consumption to stuff the emotional and physical congestion that is trying to surface. As previously mentioned, avoidance strategies can become a complex web of intertwined patterns – in other words, we use whatever works to help us feel in control and "normal." So when you resist the temptation to numb out through eating a bag of cookies on auto-pilot, you give your body time to process physical congestion by freeing your metabolism to clean house rather than digest new food, while simultaneously allowing any suppressed emotions to surface that you may have been tempted to stuff.

Stick with it. On the other side of cravings for food and drink lies freedom and inspiration – in short, a higher vibrational energy that's a thousand times more nourishing than anything you could consume.

To summarize, each alchemical transformation – that is, each time you delay any avoidance strategy to the point of discomfort or craving – you integrate a piece of your suppressed psyche and move closer to essentialization.

Chapter 7
Shed

As the alchemical substance of spiritual energy rises up within you and life-depleting avoidance strategies are discontinued, layers of condensed energy loosen, transmute, and are finally released. What's left, however, is the "housing" – the mental, emotional, and physical templates that attract and contain the repressed energy. Shedding involves letting go of the patterns that hold the suppressed energy in place. If we don't deliberately and mindfully let these patterns go, new congestion will again accumulate. These patterns include the ways in which we deal with our emotions, inaccurate belief systems, stories we tell ourselves, and ineffective ways we relate to others. Here are some examples of specific belief and behavior patterns that continue to attract more congestion:

- Negative thoughts about money

- Believing oneself to be a victim

- Spending time around unsupportive people

- Ongoing power struggles

- Emotional eating

These patterns form over extended periods of time, and if not deliberately transformed, will attract more of the same. Shedding is an extension of the alchemy phase, only deeper. Alchemically burning off old congestion requires us to abstain from our avoidance strategies, while shedding the patterns involves going within and finishing the job by making sure the internal tendencies dissolve as well. Take the example of a poor person winning the lottery. The presence of poverty in their lives is replaced with riches for a time. However, unless they actually change how they think and behave with money, their winnings will be squandered and they will end up in the same position as before.

Also, consider the woman in an emotionally abusive relationship who eventually musters up the strength to leave. Even if she grieves and heals the trauma and abuse, she still needs to go a step further and change how she sees herself and relates to others or she will attract the same type of person. I saw this happen over and over as a therapist in a domestic violence shelter. I've also experienced it myself. As a teenager I fell in love with a young man who later turned abusive. I stayed with him for many years. I finally broke up with him and mourned the years I had lost and the pain I endured. Even after that however, I chose another emotionally abusive partner.

I had begun working on my self-esteem, and luckily it took me only half the time to end that relationship… progress. But a couple years later, my heart opened again to a man who had these same tendencies, only this time I ended it immediately – after about one month. It has never come up again, even years later, because my love for myself has grown and I don't spend time around people who are not able to be loving and kind. But time alone doesn't erase these patterns, it requires internal transformation, as it is our energy that attracts others into our lives and only when we change at an energetic level will we attract different people. Until we fully embrace our own evolution (by not delaying it through the use of avoidance strategies), we will always be presented with situations that test our progress. But as you continue to walk toward yourself rather than away, these patterns all but vanish and the space is filled with only light and the luscious flavor of your essence.

Cognitive Constellations

By now most of us are aware that repetitive thoughts create forms - thought forms – which attract life energy and mold it into the shape of the form. These energized templates eventually manifest as physical reality and, over time, overlap with other templates to form a *cognitive constellation* – a group of interrelated thought patterns that take on a life of their own.

Take for example Sue, who has a victim mentality. Many separate thoughts feed this pattern of victimization. Sue doesn't like how she's treated at work; she constantly complains about her financial situation; and it is common to hear her woes about being unlucky at love. Each of these separate thoughts feed energy to the constellation until it becomes a powerful mass that demands, and thereby attracts this low level victim energy to keep itself going.

Sue could potentially enter therapy and uncover the childhood issue of emotional abuse and shame that her mother liked to bestow upon her. She could even experience these old feelings, speak to her (imagined) mother in a chair beside her, tell her how she felt as a little girl, and write a letter for closure. She may feel relief after finally coming to terms with what happened. This is wonderful – she has released the emotional congestion around being a victim. However, on the way home from the therapist's office, she gets stopped by a police officer for going through a yellow light that turned red. Within moments of getting home, Sue calls her sister to complain about the injustice of it all, citing the law that if a driver is more than half way through the intersection when it turns red, it's legal.

BAM – the constellation has been fed a new dose of victim energy. It is essential to refine and release old emotional residue through the process of alchemy, whether it be initiated in a therapist's office or surface during an argument with your spouse. However, complete integration of the psyche requires that we also transform the thought patterns that attract and contain the emotional energy. I call this shedding because, in this phase, layers of insecurity, constricting patterns and ego literally fall away, leaving us lighter, more transparent and more integrated.

In order to support the shedding process it is necessary to identify the specific cognitive constellations or self-defeating patterns that drive you to repeat the same mistakes in thinking over and over. You'll remember our discussion about the internal tension that comes from the need for homeostasis and the desire to transform and renew. We have a tendency to hold on to the status quo, even if it is not healthy. Yet, the status quo increasingly divides the presenting self from the essential self, choking off our life force.

The need for homeostasis – to preserve the landscape of the psyche, even when it is destructive - results in the energy entity (constellation) resisting its own death. This explains why, even when we want to desperately transform a self-defeating pattern, we often can't.

"I *will not* raid the refrigerator tonight. *Absolutely not.* I am strong – in control. I will eat a salad and exercise." Evening comes around and you find yourself walking to the fridge, zombie-like, and eat whatever is there like you are out of your mind – literally. This pattern is part physical: you crave the heavy energy vibration of excess food to avoid going into detox mode (physical shedding), and part emotional: an addiction to guilt. Nevertheless, the pattern itself does not want to die, so it takes over and *you* lose control. Until now that is. Once we understand how all this works, we are empowered to take control of ourselves and endure the severe discomfort of detox, emotional alchemy and dying patterns.

In the case of emotional eating and all other compulsive consumption, the cognitive constellation at work contains the belief that one has a lack of will power (life force that has reached the solar plexus and accumulated enough strength to override lower level, impulsive choices). Therefore, in addition to invoking the power of alchemy by resisting the urge to give in to cravings, thoughts of continuous "failure" need to be replaced with the idea that slip-ups are simply a mistake and offer an opportunity for improvement. This tends to be more behaviorally oriented than the deep down and firmly rooted belief about one's "weak" character or fundamental lack of will power.

Transforming cognitive constellations is part action and part thought. Do not underestimate the importance of identifying these constellations. That, in itself, activates the power of awareness to shine a light on them each time they are activated. Unconscious patterns cannot live long in the light of awareness. As you mindfully engage in formerly compulsive habits, you tame your inner animal and allow spiritual energy to rise up to your belly and fill you with the power to consciously make life enhancing choices. Ultimately we want life energy to circulate freely up and down the spine without being prematurely released through self-defeating behaviors or getting blocked by emotional or physical congestion. Feeling the burn of a craving is your path to freedom. Along with the emotional and physical work of releasing congestion and blocks, you can address the pattern mentally by affirming a new belief such as, "*I act in my own best interest.*" While changing the way you think is the key to transforming cognitive constellations, we teach ourselves who we are through a combination of right thought and right action. With each piece of suppressed energy that's integrated or released, more pure life energy will be able to flow through your body, showering you with inner peace, well being, and increased power to act on your own behalf.

Emotional Patterns

In addition to shedding the cognitive constellations or beliefs that keep us stuck, most of us have *emotional patterns* we need to shed. These patterns are entwined with cognitive constellations and can have a serious hold on the psyche. Take for example, anger. Jason has an explosive temper. He can hold it together for a while, but something inevitably triggers him and he launches into a verbal attack that leaves his victim filled with poison. Jason is "over it" a little while later, but the person or object of his rage is not. Common sense would tell us that Jason's tendency to be a time-bomb comes from repressed anger that needs to be released. While this is true, and the anger can be transmuted through the alchemical process described in the previous chapter, Jason also needs to release the *pattern* of "snapping" when his energy gets low. This requires mindfulness and the willingness to release the pattern one incident at a time. Being aware of the bigger picture is the first step: Each time he explodes, rather than release hostile energy, he accumulates more. The outburst will certainly feel like a release, but in reality the intense energy is simply repressed further as a result of "taking a piece" of the other person. The incident reinforces the pattern and more rage energy accumulates in Jason's body.

Secondly, Jason needs to bring awareness into each moment he feels the pressure of frustration starting to build-up within him. This is tough. It requires taking responsibility for his actions and behaviors. Through breathing and self-talk he can learn to handle each situation more diplomatically as it comes up. Jason can affirm his ability to handle situations appropriately by saying to himself, "I handle situations appropriately and effectively." By changing his thought *and* actions, he will begin to teach himself a new lesson about who he is and how he behaves.

Physical Habits

Sometimes a pattern appears to be primarily physical. Say for example, alcoholism. Many people turn to alcohol as a way to avoid inner *dis-ease*. When alcohol becomes a way of coping with everyday challenges, the energy builds up inside. On top of the emotional congestion lies the physical toxins from more "spirits" than the liver can effectively metabolize. When a person stops drinking excessively, the physical toxins are released, followed by the emotional congestion underneath. But even deeper than physical and emotional congestion is the pattern of avoidance. It is not enough to replace alcohol with sugar, television or work. We ultimately need to take a sober look at ourselves. For those who have been perennially distracted, this will be fairly uncomfortable. The important point here is to distinguish the energy congestion from the pattern itself. You can pull a weed, but if you don't get the root, it will grow back.

These patterns become a part of who we are – so much so that it can be difficult to recognize their existence. Whether mental, emotional or physical, these habits are attempts at responding to life's challenges. We can let all of our unhealthy patterns go with love, because they only exist in order to compensate for the lack of life energy which is supposed to be flowing freely. Transforming these patterns creates more space for life, and when enough life gets through, we have no need to compensate with self-defeating behaviors.

Physical detoxification – releasing toxins and physical congestion by fasting, clean eating or simply taking breaks from your favorite indulgences – is one of the best things you can do to support the process of shedding. Physical congestion and emotional congestion tend to overlap and intertwine. You'll notice that when your body is releasing the effects of sugar and caffeine that the common detox symptoms of head aches and low energy will be accompanied by unexpected feelings of sadness, anger or grief. This is good – your body is releasing congestion that you've potentially carried years.

We all have thought patterns (cognitive constellations), emotional congestion and physical toxins to release. Shedding these deep patterns requires deliberate attention and action. The rewards are increased energy flow, lightness in your cells and further integration of the psyche.

Chapter 8
Embody

As we move toward the last two phases of essentialization, discomfort is replaced with a sense of adventure as blockages burn off and our essence comes to the surface. You who are ushering in an era of unprecedented peace have cultivated a relationship with your spiritual core **(charge),** and are letting go of avoidance strategies in order to develop the will necessary to contain and express your light **(alchemy).** You are mindful of any deeper patterns that need released **(shed)** and are now ready to claim the real you **(embody).**

Embodying your essence – your one-of-a-kind blend of unique flavors, colors and textures – is the next step. What's your flavor? Are you spicy, mellow, fresh or earthy? Do you move like the wind or are you sturdy like a tree trunk? Do you flow like a river or are you tranquil like a still lake? If you were a color would you be a warm shade of orange or a cool blue?

You are an essential piece of the humanity puzzle. The only way to take your rightful place is to show up fully as yourself.

Completing the puzzle of humanity by being fully yourself is the most important job you have as a human being. This is the way we bring our light into the world. By reading this book you have taken a huge step toward claiming your unique and fully integrated self and expressing it as the light that it is. Your fully expressed essence demonstrates peace in the world because it is undivided and not fighting against itself.

Tragically, those who fully accept and embrace themselves are the exception. This is largely due to socialization. We as a society elevate the "ideal" to the point that people who do not fit this narrow image often feel the need to hold back. We do what we can to fit in – have plastic surgery, try to earn lots of money, seek jobs that are prestigious even if we despise them. But the cost of trying to contort ourselves into some abstract image of ideal is tremendous. Going back to the humanity puzzle metaphor, if you could visualize the puzzle piece of a person trying to fit in, it would look mostly dark with a spec or two colored in. The spec is a drop of their light – the part they are willing to show. The rest is hidden or buried. Rejecting any part of oneself means being only a partial piece of this grand puzzle, leaving all of humanity incomplete. It is our duty to embrace who we are, whether we think it is "ideal" or not. It is equally important to help others do the same, for if they are not complete, neither are we.

Discovering Your Brilliance

The reader of this book is likely in touch with her unique essence – part of which is a fierce, yet humble warrior willing to embark on the most radical path to peace that exists. And yet, we need to take it further. There cannot be any part of your essence left untouched or it will be projected outward and chased. *Remember: anything suppressed is projected outward.* This includes your baggage as well as your brilliance.

Because it is nearly impossible to see one's suppressed essence directly, let's look for it indirectly by asking some questions to identify where it's being projected.

Who do you love? No really, what actor would rock your world if you were to run into him or her? Which author, scientist or business person do you seek to emulate? What musician would you follow to the end of the earth?

There are clues in the answers to these questions. The various qualities of your essence are either embodied or projected. When you embody a quality, you enjoy and celebrate others who have similar gifts. Appreciating someone's talent without your essence being projected onto them is natural, but if you're experiencing all out adoration, fixation, or dare we say, a little obsession – the person likely embodies a quality within you that you have not yet claimed.

I know a woman named Benny. As a young girl, she played the piano and sang in church. Even as a child, this vibrant leader inspired all those around her. As the years passed however, Benny realized that she had some issues with the church and broke away. In addition to leaving the church, she walked away from her music. In her twenties, she discovered Tori Amos. Along with listening to Amos all the time, Benny attended every concert she could – always with the goal to connect with Amos at her customary "Meet and Greet." Later, Benny reclaimed her musical side, writing songs and playing the piano for loved ones. Benny also realized that it wasn't only Amos' music that pulled her, but the strength and confidence behind it. As Benny reclaimed her voice and worked to integrate the strength and confidence she had as a child, the draw to Amos shifted from a magnetic pull to a gentle draw to a musician she "adores." This is the typical progression of someone who initially projects a part of their essence onto another and then integrates it over time. The fixation turns to admiration as one embodies the very quality formerly sought in another.

This same projection/chase dynamic occurs frequently with couples. We are attracted to those who possess qualities that we need to cultivate within ourselves. A person who under-expresses may find he's attracted to a woman who is outgoing, and perhaps, over-expressive. Ideally, each is able to integrate both sides of the continuum over time and be able to act whatever way is most appropriate to a given situation. The evolution of the couple usually goes one of two ways, each of them either integrates more of the opposite quality, thereby becoming more well-rounded individuals, or the couple polarizes, becoming even more extreme in their differences. In the case of the under-expressive man and the over-expressive woman, the man ends up hardly speaking at all and the woman goes overboard and does the talking for the both of them, whereas with integration, the man learns to speak up a little more and the woman learns to be quiet when needed. The goal of essentialization is to integrate all aspects of oneself and be whole rather than find someone who's the opposite and settle for being half of one's potential.

Projecting love onto another prior to allowing it to fill you up first is another dynamic that arises out of a divided psyche and happens with almost everyone entering an intimate relationship. In this case, the love or life energy within that is meant to rise up and move outward through the heart center is given away prematurely as it is projected onto another from your core. It feels fine and even fairytale-like when your partner is pouring it back to you. This honeymoon dance is not sustainable however, just like the high from alcohol is impossible to sustain over time. Eventually, one must go within to receive genuine nourishment, which is the only lasting source of energy. If continuing to drink leads to a hang-over, continuing to expect recycled love from your partner leads to power struggles. Eventually, your partner has a bad day or feels drained and doesn't have enough energy left to share. You get angry.

"All I've done for you and you can't even support me right now!"

The power struggle can last hours or even days until both become exhausted and go their separate ways. They can then recharge from within, return to sanity, and come back together in a peaceful place – only to have the pattern start all over again: Projection—high—disconnect—power struggle— distance (a.k.a.: break-up to make-up). The opportunity contained within this relational entwinement is integration of one's spiritual energy. We sometimes call this self-love, but this phrase is misleading because really it is the absence of self-rejection. It is the decision to allow life to fill you up, burn through blocks and extend through your heart freely, without expectation, manipulation or reward. When we are full to the point of life naturally extending outward, we don't need anything back. And if we feel a situation is unhealthy in some way, we act appropriately and sometimes leave, but do not seek to manipulate for power or energy because we have our own unending source.

Sometimes, only one person is able to pull back their projection by discontinuing the relational avoidance strategy – in this case, by refusing to engage in the power struggle, thereby allowing life to transform one's inner landscape. When this occurs, one person evolves and the other does not, which often leads to the relationship ending if the other person continues to avoid his or her own work.

Discontinuing a relational avoidance strategy can be very difficult but is the only way to reclaim or integrate the part of oneself projected onto another. Success involves refusing to act the way you always have. When you crave love from another person and refuse to manipulate or fight to get it, it feels lonely, desperate and painful. But when the fog lifts, you are clear inside and can see the relationship for what it is.

Additionally, you have strengthened the connection to your essence and burned away some blocks. This can take many times of refusing to initiate or engage in the power struggle. Eventually, you'll be able to observe your partner's behavior without it pushing your buttons. That's when you know you have made significant progress toward inner integration.

Unconditional love – the level of relationship to which most of us aspire – is possible only when a person has *complete* self-acceptance. As we've said, everything suppressed is projected outward and then sought indirectly through the object or person onto which it's projected. How can we love a person with no strings attached if we are dependent upon them to deliver us back to ourselves? In this sense, the alchemy and embody phases of essentialization are two sides of the same coin, with shedding being a natural outcome of both. Once we start clearing out emotional congestion, we can begin to embody our light. Your essence is primarily made of love with some spice mixed in for flavor, and embodying it requires that you receive your own love directly rather than projecting it onto a loved one only to chase it. Once you fully receive yourself, sharing it with others is the sweetest reward.

Envy and Desire

There's another way to identify your suppressed brilliance/essence: What qualities do you envy in others? What do others have that you desire? Do you feel jealous of anyone? We do not feel jealous or envious of qualities that we do not already possess in potential. If you are the scientific type, you probably don't envy artists. But if you have untapped artistic potential, you could very well envy someone who is a fully embodied artist.

What kind of cars do you like? You know the saying that men with big trucks are trying to compensate for something that they lack? There may be some truth to that – but perhaps it's not what you think… They may be drawn to big trucks for the strength and power they represent as a way to help them integrate their own. What about a middle-aged woman driving a convertible? A convertible represents freedom and fun, something many women crave after decades of caretaking. There is nothing wrong with using external objects to help us claim attributes of ourselves that need cultivated, as long as we're working on embodying these qualities rather than simply chasing them in objects.

Any desire you have, whether it's to have more money, get in better shape, or learn to play the piano comes from life wanting to fulfill an untapped area of potential within you. All desires are therefore completely valid, as they arise out of life seeking fuller expression. Many of us judge our desires as being superficial or non-important, but perhaps we need to revisit life's purpose – to extend itself. Flowers, for example are gorgeous, displaying perfect petals in vibrant colors. What if the flower was to only partially bloom and then think to itself, "At least I'm healthy… there's no need to be greedy and want perfection."

We are each perfect in our essence and that essence seeks full expression. That's not to say that perfection involves having a flawless form, rather it refers to full function of potential in every area of our lives. Desire is life's way of pro-creating. Procreation is not just about having babies. It involves every kind of creation. Sexual desire propels us toward biological procreation and the desire for more money propels us toward fulfilling our financial potential in the world. All desires come from life and are therefore sacred and healthy if used to create more life.

Whenever I see someone similar to myself living at her potential, I become inspired (in-spirit). I "catch" the life she emanates, which encourages me on my own path. I recommend that any time you notice a quality in someone that you envy, instead of thinking, "I envy that…" You turn it around and say, "I am that…" Because the truth is, you are what you admire, whether you perceive it or not. As the saying goes, *it takes one to know one.*

Celebrating the unique qualities in those around us serves to accelerate our own unfolding. By admiring the particular and beautiful ways life displays itself in others we teach ourselves that our unique peculiarities are beautiful as well. Additionally, noticing what makes another person special is the biggest gift we can give to them. To be truly seen is rare indeed and when you take the time to really see someone, they feel it, whether you say it out loud or not.

Complete Self-Acceptance

Essentialization is not limited to spiritual integration, although claiming your unique essence is at the heart of this transformative process. The journey to essentialization is not complete until you accept and embody all aspects of yourself. This includes your thoughts/beliefs, emotions, and physical body, along with your spirit. There is no place where your spirit is not, therefore if you reject *any* aspect of yourself then a piece of your essence is buried. It might help to think of your spiritual/mental/emotional/physical self as a continuum of your essence progressing from pure energy to more and more concrete manifestations of that same energy.

You'll notice when looking at your brothers and sisters who are well on the path to essentialization that they emanate a striking level of self-acceptance. These folks have imperfections just like the rest of us, but they have learned to accept and love these imperfections as a part of their unique nature. In turn, you'll find them endearing too. You'll see their distinct features and quirky personality characteristics as beautiful, maybe even desirable. The woman with the big nose becomes exotic. Big hips become sensual. A loud laugh is contagious, and so on. We only judge people when they are judging themselves. We intuitively perceive the areas of self-rejection and without even realizing what's happening, add our judgments into the mix.

As a result of this level of self-acceptance, essentialized men and women are complete in a way that inspires us. They are guided and fueled by their spiritual natures. They are emotionally clear and refined – not ruled by buried emotional landmines. They have awareness of their thoughts and exercise mental discipline to ensure that they are productive. Finally, they have complete acceptance of their bodies which allows them to be comfortable in their own skin – sensual, sexual, physically active and enjoying life's pleasures. This level of evolution does not emphasize the spiritual at the expense of the physical, as essentialization cannot be a reality until we are wholly integrated.

If committed to essentialization, life will present you with opportunities to reclaim each buried piece of you. Your part involves making the sincere commitment to wholeness and then saying "yes" to opportunities for integration as they come up. The buried aspects of yourself will most often be reflected back to you by another person. This is usually pretty uncomfortable. For if these parts of you were easy to look at then they would not be buried. When someone says something that makes you feel bad, consider it a gift. It just means there is more of you that *you* need to love. Once you have complete self-acceptance (have become essentialized), another's words or actions will not trigger the kind of pain we feel when someone has "hit a nerve." Instead of reacting with the defensiveness required to keep the ego intact, you will be able to respond with self love, and set appropriate boundaries. Those of us who accept ourselves completely choose only loving people to be around, as we are ultimately treated the same way we treat ourselves.

Embodying your essence – embracing who you really are and bringing it all to the surface – is the blossoming stage of essentialization. Identifying the different qualities that make you unique is a process that unfolds over time. Like a flower – if you are willing – life brings you into full bloom.

Here is a list of questions to help you fully embody your essence:

1. What qualities do you admire most in others?

2. What are you most attracted to in your partner or in a potential partner?

3. Who is your favorite musician or actor and what qualities draw you to him or her?

4. What makes you green with envy?

5. What pushes your buttons?

Reflecting on these questions will help you uncover the parts of yourself that have been pushed aside. Fully embodying your essence takes time, but once you've claimed and accepted all that you are, your projections of division give way to a wholly integrated mind that can extend forth in peace.

You are now ready to move on to the final stage of essentialization: expressing yourself in all your glory.

Chapter 9
Express

We've reached the final stage of essentialization and the pinnacle of this sacred journey. Expression is your birthright, and occurs naturally as you become more integrated and peaceful inside. It's impossible for life to fully emerge from a divided and congested psyche, as integration is required to shine this brightly. Prior to this point, the divided psyche has had no choice but to project itself outward, only to be perceived as good/evil, democrat/republican and us/them divisions in the world. Additionally, the emotions repressed through the use of avoidance strategies (anger, hurt, frustration, sadness, etc.) have fueled these projections, causing us to intensely react to them as if they were completely separate from us. This dysfunctional way of avoiding our own inner demons by projecting them onto other people, religions and countries threatens our very existence, and it is for this reason you have been called to travel the path of essentialization – a path that is sometimes dark and filled with cobwebs and monsters – yet leads you home.

Full expression requires that you've traveled the first four legs of the journey: 1) Charge, 2) Alchemy, 3) Shed, 4) Embody, as preparation for sharing your essence and light with the world. As an integrated psyche, you'll still perceive imbalance and wrongdoing, but instead of reacting to it with vicious emotion and adding to the problem, you'll pour the light of awareness onto the person or situation, helping restore it to health and balance.

Levels of Expression

For many years I believed that they only way to change the world was to reach millions of people. Many of us fall into this mistaken belief. The truth is, there is only one way to heal the world and that is to become integrated and whole yourself.

This brings us back to the most profound concept presented in this book: It is not your words, thoughts or even deeds that heal the world, but your presence alone. One fully integrated man or woman pours light into this dim world by simply existing. It is not necessary to feed the hungry or shelter the homeless, although those of us on this path frequently do so. Charity of all kinds is supremely important and needs to happen if we are to lift everyone up. One's basic needs must be met or preoccupations with survival will outweigh even the desire for inner peace. However, *world peace* doesn't come from lending a hand, it comes from demonstrating peace – perhaps we can demonstrate peace while lending a hand? The bottom line is that whether you choose to live a quiet life tending your garden or decide to run for political office in order to effect change, your presence outweighs your deeds. So, in addition to doing whatever we do in this world – raising children, providing accounting services or making music – we must cultivate a peaceful presence within ourselves if we want to fundamentally change the landscape of the collective psyche. Just as there are no unnecessary pieces in a puzzle, no *one* person's presence is more important than any other. If any one of us is tormented inside, that piece of the puzzle is not lit up, resulting in the entire puzzle being compromised. While healing can only come about one person at a time, each of us who lights up from the inside creates more momentum toward an overall shift.

Expressing Your Emotions

If alchemy burns through old emotional residue that constricts life flow, emotional expression keeps you clear as your light increases. Emotions are simply life energy moving through you at different vibratory rates. Some are heavy and slow, while others are light and fast moving. It is the heavier one's that tend to get stuck, which is understandable because processing them doesn't feel good. The heaviness, however is only exaggerated when we resist these feelings. Learning to express all feelings – positive and negative – is critical to staying clear and open.

A friend of mine recently shared how he views emotional expression, stating, "I don't feel the need to express things that I can process on my own in a few minutes or an hour, but when something sticks with me, I have to deal with it or it starts burning in my chest."

I thought this was well put, as choosing to suppress emotions rather than feel them causes the energy to turn against us like cancer cells. Although, as my friend described, processing emotions doesn't always need to involve communication with another. We can process intense emotions any number of ways, such as through journaling or exercising. Sometimes, however, emotions "stick" with us until expressed to the person involved or a neutral third party.

Keeping emotional energy flowing is critical to inner peace – and to doing our part in creating world peace. Emotional congestion is a form of inner division because in order to store it, we must be in denial that it is even there. This leads to having an unconscious shadow side that's projected outward, thereby magnifying conflict in the world around you.

While expressing difficult emotions can be scary, sharing love with others can cause us to feel even more vulnerable. Despite the perceived risk of putting ourselves "out there," the benefits of doing so are well worth it. Love, expressed in all its forms, fills you up, increasing your vibratory rate before extending outward. The world needs heart-based energy now more than ever, and loving life and other people is the only way this sweet nectar is shared. The risk (and reason many of us shy away from expressing boundless love) is that it may not be reciprocated. However, when the energy of love fills us up and spontaneously extends to another, it is truly unconditional and doesn't require reciprocation. It is only when we give love from the solar plexus or power center that it has strings attached. A good way to test if the love you're about to give is unconditional is to ask yourself, "Will I be okay if this person doesn't respond in kind?" If the answer is yes, then feel free to love them up! If the answer is no, then love yourself a little more first, and when you are full, this precious energy will joyously and freely flow forth.

Cultivating the full range of emotional expression is an art that each of us needs to master if we are sincere about our commitment to inner and outer peace. Doing so is truly liberating, releasing any self-imposed bondage in favor of fully expressing your essence.

Expressing Your Brilliance

In addition to fully sharing your emotions, there is another level of expression, which, when activated, increases the velocity of light moving through you. This level involves sharing your brilliance with the world. Each of us has a brand of brilliance shared by no one, *and the world desperately needs all of it.* The idea that we have competing talents is pervasive in our collective consciousness, leading us to the mistaken belief that our brilliance is not needed because there is so much out there already. This is a false and ultimately poisoning belief. It is only when we reject a part of ourselves in an attempt to try to be like others that our brilliance becomes generic and diluted.

think. Seeing these folks makes you want to connect to your own brilliance. In fact, those who express their essence nullify competition, replacing it with contagious inspiration. Just think of the last time you met someone who fully embodied and expressed their unique brand of life. Even when another's brilliance lies in a completely different area than your own, their presence brings you closer to your potential. These people are my heroes. They are versions of you and me – everyday men and women who have decided to risk it all in order to be true to themselves and fill their piece of the humanity puzzle. Brilliance comes in all shapes and sizes, but the one common element of those who choose to express their essence is a profound sense of inner peace. Inner peace *is* the feeling associated with the full embodiment and expression of life. It is only at this stage that one becomes a portal of peace.

Chapter 10
From Inner Peace
to World Peace

Those of us dedicated to doing our part in creating a more peaceful world must reclaim inner peace as a priority above all else. Western society has somehow lost the value of inner peace in our extreme pursuit of achievement, wealth and other external goals. Some of the wealthiest people I know have shared that despite having achieved success and material abundance, something is still missing in their lives. That something is inner peace. The end never justifies the means, for how can we rush toward a goal – fragmented and distracted – and then expect to all of a sudden have peace when we arrive? Peace is both the outcome of essentialization and the way in which we live our lives. It is the result of life energy flowing through you as it is designed to do. This book is a step-by-step guide to true and lasting peace. If putting inner peace above all else feels selfish, it is probably because of the wide-spread confusion about what's important, often delivered by the media via marketing strategies aimed at getting products sold.

Peace as a Priority

It is time to re-prioritize our values, putting inner peace at the top of the list. When each choice made is based on the question of whether it will bring you peace, everything else falls into place. Using peace as a guide, you march to the beat of life's drum, instead of your small self or ego. Being in sync with life benefits the whole – our relationships, our environment and the world – because we cannot become more light-filled without sharing it with others.

Choosing peace doesn't always feel good. For example, there are times when it's right to end a relationship, but the choice to do so brings heart-wrenching pain and sadness. Below the hurricane of emotions, however, is a sense of deep down peace. Choosing peace is going with the will of life, and life always brings stormy seasons and droughts. But there are only two choices to be made, 1) hold on to what you know, resisting life's seasons of transformation, or 2) surrender to life, facing all that you are *not* in order to become all that you *are*. The first choice is an attempt to avoid death, because once we stop running from life, it burns through the false self, which involves a part of us dying. But why avoid death? We all have to face it someday. Why not jump in now and live fully rather than avoid the inevitable, only to be among the walking dead? The second choice is the choice of warriors – those willing to fight for life. If you are reading these words you are a soldier. You may not be ready to discontinue your favorite avoidance strategy today or even tomorrow, but you will be soon. Just continue to connect to your spiritual core each day, allowing it to fill you up and give you the courage and strong foundation to withstand this transformative journey.

The planet needs your light now more than ever before, however it can only absorb the healing rays of your spirit as it passes through you, which just happens to feel good! So rest assured that there is no higher pursuit than inner peace – yes, you benefit in that you get your life back – but everyone else benefits as well. Your peace directly translates to peace in the world in three ways:

1. By reclaiming your buried self and allowing life to burn through your blocks, you become integrated inside and no longer project division onto the world.

2. By putting inner peace above all else, you demonstrate peace, becoming a contagious source of deep down calm, which is both healing and nourishing to those around you.

3. By sharing your brilliance – no matter how quirky or original – you increase the volume of light moving through your body, thereby bringing much needed light into the world.

Divided Versus Essentialized

Going through the process of essentialization gives us an orientation toward life that unites rather than divides. We see everything through a different lens – one that is whole. The perspective of wholeness is like looking through the eyes of God. The vision itself emphasizes our similarities rather than our differences, thereby fostering solutions that are fundamentally healing. To give you an idea of the differences between the divided and essentialized psyche, below is a list of attributes for each.

Divided	Essentialized
Ideal Forms	Beauty in Variety
Win/Lose	Win/Win
Scarcity	Abundance
Competition	Synergy
Sameness	Uniqueness
Consumption	Expression
Superficial	Authentic
Guarded	Transparent
Rigid Standards	Creativity
Judgment	Compassion

Within the essentialized psyche, the right and left brain are integrated as well as the feminine and masculine aspects of oneself. Black and white thinking is replaced with the ability to see multiple perspectives. When we embrace all the faces of our essence, the whole is contained within us. This is not to say that we don't have our unique strengths and preferences, only that we are not suppressing any parts of ourselves that get projected onto others. Total integration means that we are able to look at a violent criminal, and think to ourselves, "He must feel so desperate and disconnected" rather than seeing him as an "evil monster." We will naturally approach all the conflicts in the world in a way that invokes light rather than feeding darkness when we ourselves are whole (holy) and full of light.

The Final Vision

This brings us back to the incredible vision that led to the writing of this book: Our beautiful globe with beams of light streaming out from its surface, as one by one, each of us opens up from the inside. This process gains momentum as the increasing light inspires more courageous souls to walk the path of essentialization. This was the vision for *Portals of Peace*. It is my hope that you make this path your own, starting from exactly where you are. The world is waiting for each and every one of us to embark on our own adventure where we explore the most uninviting territory before getting to the other side where beauty and peace prevail.

Light is winning, so much so that this process is easier than it has ever been. Being enlightened is no longer reserved for a select few, but is available to all of us for the taking. To find your guru, simply look in the mirror. Many teachers – living here on earth and beyond – are available to help you, but your best teacher is the one inside you that yearns to extend itself in light.

Understanding the bigger picture is the hardest part. Now that you know why you sometimes sabotage your growth despite good intentions, you are armed with the tools necessary to transcend any challenges you formerly faced. All we've been delaying is our own inevitable transformation. As more and more of us release our spirit and light into the world, darkness turns to illumination, assisting those who are still lost to find their way home. Together, we experience peace as we never have. You truly are the light of the world.